# A Wildflower Creation

Understanding Einstein

I'm trying to understand Einstein
To pull the stitching through
Because I feel in all his work
There is something true
And it's not made of weather
It's not made of tides
It is of the nature
Of that which abides

Gravity

What holds the stars in the grip of the sky
How do they keep their balance to refract my eye
And is there a heavenly force
That holds them tight throughout the course
Of apparent time and space
A symphony you cannot chase
A magnetic hum
And is God beating that drum
As all of creation sings in harmony
Like a bird upon a tree
To hold and catch a single note
Just one more genius that I quote

The Equation of Us

Can I write the equation of us
Is this something that I can trust
And I balance both sides so it is even
And I loved you without a reason

Soul Song

Are we all buzzing atoms
And you share my soul song
To love you
Could never be wrong

Opal Eyes

His eyes were like opals
Shining at me
And I can't explain
Who I'm meant to be
And he's perfectly lovely
To see through the rain
And I've been wondering
What is there to gain
And I'd hold your hand
And I'd sing you a song
But you're not the place
I really belong
Though I love you
Now that much is true
I don't know how to put words
To what I feel for you

The Half Life

My ardent heart
Comes away and tears me apart
Like I asked it to
I told it what to do
If I hid out in compromise
If I agreed to the lies
It shows me the way
By making it unbearable to stay
In the half light
It's never alright
To be just okay
So I let my heart lead the way
Back to home
I know I am not alone

I never find that piece of knowledge
That keeps eluding me
It's like my brain is searching
For an answer that is key
But is the consciousness
Really what I am
It moves without a why
It moves without a plan

Is this a hoax, is this a ruse
Is it made up, the path that I choose
Because I've always been cut out
For less travelled by
Is that an old oak
Just give me an aye

Relativity

How heat can feel like heaven on a cold night
How I could be saved by the beautiful light
How something pure and undefined
Could illuminate a darkened mind
It's all relative, you see
It didn't just happen to me
But all of creation in this body and soul
Like a grain of sand reflecting the whole
It's all relative, like a microcosm of the complete
The days when I fell at your feet
Only to stand up tall
And maybe there never was a wall
Just confusion and misunderstanding
It's all relative, I guess
And you never put me to the test
We'll work it out
Because love is what we are about
It's all relative, like gravity
Pulling you back to me
As it holds the stars in a midnight sky
We revolve and I don't know why
It's all relative, you say
And for once I am okay
With your hand in mine
We walk through both space and time
To find love
Sent from above
A white dove
That's what I'm thinking of

Sublimation

Sharing my frozen glance
With someone else
And am I done
Melting myself
As I block of ice
Against your warm
You move with the weight
Of a thunderstorm
And your rain
Turns the cold
I'm running through
Fields of gold

The Quantum Realm

The quantum reality of a black hole
Is the singularity of my soul
Where everything loses all meaning
And you just wake up from dreaming
As the world of duality collapses
And I am firing on all synapses

Unified Field Theory

If there's a unified field
I call it love
From below to above
The substratum
That contains all things
An awareness
In hearts it sings

I smile because I feel you
In the sky and in the air
Though we haven't talked in years
Somehow you're still there

Holy Dance

I love the boy in the band
And he held my hand
For an instant or two
Like a guitar pick he strums along to
And my heart and my soul
Will be with him til we get old
And after if we have the chance
I think this life's a holy dance
Transcendental
It's on another level
It's a different vibe
It is the feeling
Of being alive

Losing myself in the emo scene
And is this just part of the dream

Divine Intervention

The pain is a form of divine intervention
All that's kept hidden that I dare not mention
It's a fierce grace
That makes me run and hide my face
Til I've pulled myself up by my bootstraps
And got out those ancient maps
That lead me back to the core
The place where I don't need anymore
I know it's there
And life's way of being unfair
Is to orient me
Back to how it's supposed to be
And his eyes
Show me truth without lies
I keep writing odes to the crystalline
When time was naught and he was divine
But ever free
I think I'm becoming who I'm meant to be

Am I a Biffy freak
And is that the highlight of my week

Kingdoms and Queens

We've touched before
As I said I don't love you anymore
Because to pull away was all I knew
To deal with the threat of losing you
And I know it was foolish, I know it was mean
It's just you're the kingdom and I am the queen
And you're supposed to do what I say
You didn't so I went away
And there's no road back to that place anymore
But I confess, I do adore
Everything you are and be
Could you still hold the answer to me?

Storm

I'm not in the mood to be depressed
So you can turn that music off
It's like I'm Snow White in the woods
All I'm doing is getting lost
And do you think there's a prince, in all seriousness
Or is this dreaming mind a problem to address
Because I saw you like a king
Or a mountaintop or tower
I saw you like a hero
Using their favourite power
And Storm was my favourite
As she turned her eyes about
To make the weather move
In a way you could not doubt
And fire is my sign, Aries, the ram
But it doesn't encapsulate exactly what I am
Yes I am full of flair and I am right here
With Mars as my ruler to make the spirit dear
But it says nothing about the light that's broken through
And I can see it shining in the eyes of you
And I try to look away but it's everything I see
Even though I go unnoticed, there's nothing special about me
And I am fascinated by the lines you weave
It's even more a wonder that I've come to believe
That although you're not perfect, you come pretty close
And despite my best intentions I love you the most
And you're air in the sky, you just breeze on through
I didn't mean to get so taken with the feel of you

I was so alive at seventeen
Before I got hooked on the dream

Awareness

Is it the age of darkness
Do the skies roll
And what is this speaking
To my soul
That everything
Turns out alright
It doesn't matter
About the night
That just comes falling
From the sky
As diamond points
Reach my eye
Just light from
A far distant star
And do any of you
Know who you are
Or are we just spinning
Momentum bound
As a consequence

Of sound
And there is
A way out of here
I know it coz
I've taken it dear
And I will point
Beyond the light
Into a space
That will ignite
Every fibre
Of your being
Remember to question
What you're seeing
As you are pulled
This way or that
Don't lose your balance
On the flat
Ground which
You stand upon
What's always there
It's never gone

I want to be a new born leader
Not full of the words they feed her
I want to lead the way of light
Show everyone out of the night

So what does it matter
If I am a geek
And I colour my diary
In every week
And it's all coded
Oh my God, OCD
Could you all please
Stop judging me

Am I a Fool?

The foolhardiness of my youth
And in the hospital I hugged Ruth
I never expected to see her there
I wouldn't have thought she'd even care
But she did and I met her back
Without the wings of an attack
And I don't know how I keep ending up in these places
And I'm all for creating spaces
And rooms where people can go to rest
Lord knows they put me to the test
So I'll send them flowers like it's a wedding day
I hope that will be okay

Love Poems

I didn't mean to write 10,000 love poems about the same guy
It didn't give me a reason, didn't even ask why
All I know is it's spinning a yarn from my hair
The colour of straw that is just lying there
And you could call it gold or mineral ore
It seems to be precious but I don't know what for
And am I like the miner with the celestial gem
I discover it, then go hacking again

My relationship with life
My union with you
And it is more
Than just us two

H2

Do I let my creativity flair
Or am I still hiding what's there
Because it's not the norm
Not what people do
Sit back and compose
Imaginations of you
And you're perfectly fine
You're ok, you're alright
But you shine like the diamonds
Of stars at night
And I have to say
I am my own sun
But if you were an element
You'd be hydrogen
As we would just burn
The whole night away
The darkness of space
The brightness of day

I'm moving out of the land of death
A land of time I can learn to forget

It feels like it just gets taken out of my hands
Maybe I should surrender to it
It's just like a tide or a current or flow
And I'm just going with it
Is that the Tao
The unnameable name
The feeling that's outside all definition
And a play that's not in the game

I wish I could give him up
He's like a bad drug
I keep getting high
On the hits of his love

Impersonal intimacy
I could just kiss
The person
I'm standing with

It was love at first sight
The day I met you
And the needle is pulling
The stitching through

His hair in his eyes
He's looking at me
And to some surprise
I'm looking back

Times Square

Feeling my heart beat in Times Square
I was present, yes I was there
The scent of you was in the air
And I can feel the fabric start to tear
As it all comes apart in my hands
Life is more than slipping sands
And once the heart understands
There's no room for any more well laid plans
But you're like a riff the sky plays
And you're the red clouds at the end of days
And I feel for you in so many ways
And although the love always stays
I still find myself getting mad
At you for all that you had
And yes, it leaves me feeling bad
But it's a damn sight better than the sad
You leave in your wake as the current pulls
But time's a healer and the pain dulls
As we all just get on by
And I'm glad I didn't try
To catch you when you went to leave
Freedom's in what you believe

The Infinite Darkness

I'm staring at the infinite darkness
He says that it is him
He pulls in close to kiss my lips
With his hand under my chin
And he talks to me so softly
His breath like eiderdown
I can feel myself in his arms
Just miles outside of town
And he says that I'm lovely
And deep and sincere
And for the first time in my life
I let someone come near
And see the secret garden
That is just behind the wall
He holds my hands as we walk
Through the door into it all
And to my wonder I'm not scared
To my wonder I don't mind
To my astonishment
I leave it all behind
And settle into living
In a realm beyond the stars
I don't think I'll ever figure out
Exactly what we are

Particle Physics

The particle physics that swims in my brain
It is a poet or a songbird's refrain
It is all music, all of this mathematics
And I am full of amateur dramatics
As I write my sonnets out to the sky
It's the big questions, it's all about why
And it all seems to revolve on the axis of I
I can't understand it, although I try
But Maharishi points out to find
The root of the problem in the wheel that I grind
That there is an answer to be known in truth
And this is much more than contemplations of youth

Metaphysics

Is it all metaphysical
Is it all in the air
Are you just a memory
Or were you there
In every sliver of time
That slips through my hand
Are you more than just music
To play in a band
Are you deeper than light
And more profound
You can't capture you
In any sound
Only go weaving
You through the fold
I amn't selling
Because I was sold

Its driving me off the edge of the world
Into the infinite abyss
And love is the only thing
That I cannot miss

Time moves so slow
It's almost glacial

Imagination

In my imaginary world
I'm just a girl
Who knows how to write and play
And how to make everybody's day
But in the real world
Who am I
The one who's not
Afraid to die
Because I have seen
The fabric tear
The disguise
We all wear

The dark denizens of my mind
I throw caution to the wind and leave it all behind

The Master knows where you are at all times
Like a cow with a bell round her neck, it chimes
And it must be you who jumps over the moon
In the Father's house there are many rooms

The uncertainty principle
Do I have it straight
That I never even
Had to wait

The Years of My Life

Being thirty years old and looking seventeen
But all of this is happening within the dream
And I am lucidly watching it all unfold
Or am I a pauper still searching for gold
When the diamond's in my pocket and it's always been this way
There's nothing I can glean from anything anyone could say
And I'm always brought back to the same place again
To hear the birdsong whistle through the glen

Am I just finding my identity
In being the smart one
And is all that chasing round
Not already done

I have to let go of all the pretend
And misery is not my friend

I love you
I need to write the words
Even if in all of this
They go unheard

The beauty in every pair of eyes
I see that which never dies
And is always in love with the present moment
Where do you think you're going?
Is it to work or is it to school
Don't hide away, if that's cool

I want to look deep into every soul
So I see the part that's not getting old

Stop seeking to try and tell
Everyone that I am well
Just be the change I want to see
And reveal the depths of me

I've  put all my eggs in one basket
And I can only tell the truth if you ask it

It's an edifice I've abandoned
The old tumbling stone
Leaves me with gaps
To traverse alone

I don't know how to bow down
I only know how to stand tall
And I can see the light
Through the crumbling wall

If you wish to use any of the poetry in this book please reference
www.thepoetrybook.space


Cover photo is by Alexander Andrews at Unsplash.com